Mark Ryan was born in London in 1959. After leaving school at 16 he toured in various bands including Adam and the Ants, appearing in Derek Jarman's 1977 film *Jubilee*. In the late 1980's he attended Dartington College of Arts and gained a degree in music, collaborating with the theatre department on a wide range of productions. He moved to Wales in 1991 settling in Cardiff where he worked in professional theatre as a playwright, musician and designer.

He was a prolific playwright producing work that often integrated music and song with vibrant dialogue. His work reached a wide audience including children and young people, winning acclaim and awards. *The Strange Case of Dr Jekyll and Mr Hyde as told to Carl Jung by an inmate of Broadmoor Asylum* was first performed at the Edinburgh Festival in 1997 and was The Scotsman's Five Star Pick of The Day; while *The Lazy Ant*, a play for 4 to 7 year olds, won Best Script and Best Production at the International Children's Theatre Festival in Shanghai in 2007.

Mark died in 2011 while finalising the text of his novel *Sean Tyrone*.

THE STRANGE CASE OF DR JEKYLL AND MR HYDE

AS TOLD TO CARL JUNG

BY AN INMATE OF

BROADMOOR ASYLUM

PARTHIAN

Parthian, Cardigan SA43 1ED
www.parthianbooks.com
This edition published in 2014
© estate of Mark Ryan
ISBN 978-1-906998-58-5
Cover design and typesetting by
Head & Heart Publishing Services
Printed and bound by lightningsource.com
Published with the support of the Welsh Books Council

Dedicated to Mark's children, Louis and Anna

INTRODUCTION

Mark Ryan had success with a number of adaptations of classic texts, but he was always keen to find a new and innovative way to tell the story. With *Jekyll and Hyde* he settled on the framework of an imagined Carl Jung case study. Jung was, of course, fascinated by the divided self.

The play begins with a series of interviews between Carl Jung and the incarcerated inmate, a Mr Hyde. This is the device which enables the story to be revealed. As the play develops it becomes a battle of wills and a duel of words, as the psyche of both men is dissected.

The play's lengthy title is Mark's nod to the full title of Peter Weiss' MARAT/SADE.

Jekyll and Hyde was the first of three plays which Mark Ryan wrote for Equinox Theatre. The play opened at Venue 13 at the 1997 Edinburgh Festival Fringe, before a tour of venues in Wales. The play received excellent reviews and many of the performances were sold out. The play was *The Scotsman's* Five Star, Pick of The Day.

The play was later produced by Knighthorse Theatre in San Francisco and by Sly Fox in London.

Chris Morgan
Equinox Theatre

THE STRANGE CASE OF DR JEKYLL AND MR HYDE

AS TOLD TO CARL JUNG BY AN INMATE OF BROADMOOR ASYLUM

Based on the book by Robert Louis Stevenson

First presented by Equinox Theatre at Venue 13 at the Edinburgh Festival Fringe on 10th August 1997.

Cast
JUNG   Dyfrig Morris
HYDE   James Westaway

The role of JUNG was played by Simon H. West on the tour of Wales in 1998.

Creative Team
DIRECTOR   Chris Morgan
SET DESIGN   Gerwyn Lloyd
COSTUME DESIGN   Leonie Rintler
LIGHTING DESIGN   Dave Roxburgh
STAGE MANAGER   Ally Jenkins

I

(MUSIC. THE LIGHTS COME UP SLOWLY TO REVEAL HYDE IN CHAINS. A LIGHT COMES UP DOWNSTAGE OF HYDE INTO WHICH JUNG ENTERS. AFTER A BRIEF PAUSE DURING WHICH HE SCANS THE AUDITORIUM, JUNG CLEARS HIS THROAT AND ADDRESSES THE AUDIENCE AS THOUGH DELIVERING A PUBLIC LECTURE)

JUNG: Civilisation requires us to wear a mask or 'persona'. We wear this mask when we play our part in society. A man who is a priest must play the part of a priest flawlessly at all times, for this is what society expects and demands of its members.

(GENERAL COVER ON SLOW FADE UP)

HYDE: (QUIETLY) And they came over unto the other side of the sea, into the country of the Gadarenes. And when he was come out of the ship, immediately there met him out of the tombs a man with an unclean spirit, who had his dwelling among the tombs; and no man could bind him, no, not with chains.

JUNG: But there is another side to us that is found in the

3

unconscious. This is the 'shadow'; the primitive, inferior being who wants to do everything we cannot allow ourselves to do. We are ashamed of our shadow with his uncivilised desires that, were they to be indulged, would put us beyond the pale of decent society.

HYDE: Because that he had been often bound with fetters and chains, and the chains had been plucked asunder by him, and the fetters broken in pieces; neither could any man tame him. And always, night and day, he was in the mountains, and in the tombs, crying, and cutting himself with stones.

JUNG: And so we repress him, which burdens us with such a weight of hypocrisy and deceit that we can scarcely bear it without eventually collapsing under the strain. The shadow gains in strength and vigour in the unconscious until it can no longer be held in check. At which point it bursts forth, completely overwhelming the rest of the personality.

HYDE: But when he saw Jesus afar off, he ran and worshipped him, and cried with a loud voice, and said, What have I to do with thee, thou Son of the most high God? I adjure thee by God, that thou torment me not.

JUNG: There is no shadow without the sun. It is the way of things that there be both light and dark and it is necessary for the health of the psyche that we accept the nature of its duality.

HYDE: For he said unto him, Come out of the man, thou unclean spirit. And he asked him, What is thy name? And he answered, saying, My name is Legion: for we are many.

(JUNG MOVES TOWARD HYDE, WHO SHRINKS AWAY LIKE AN ANIMAL)

JUNG: And now to our case study. (TO HYDE) Close your eyes.

(HYDE CLOSES HIS EYES)

Are you hypnotised now?

HYDE: Yes.

JUNG: But you can't be asleep, as you're talking to me.

HYDE: Yes, that's right, I'm not asleep.

JUNG: I'm now going to hypnotise you. (TO AUDIENCE) The patient, Edward H., was committed to Broadmoor Criminal Lunatic Asylum having been tried for murder but found insane. (TO HYDE) Are you asleep now? (NO ANSWER) Are you asleep? (NO ANSWER) You will be able to speak presently. Are you asleep?

HYDE: Yes.

JUNG: What do you see?

HYDE: A door.

JUNG: Is it your door?

HYDE: No.

JUNG: Is it my door?

HYDE: No.

JUNG: Is it your door?

HYDE: Yes.

JUNG: Describe it to me.

HYDE: I don't know...

JUNG: Is there a knocker? A bell?

HYDE: No.

JUNG: What colour is it?

HYDE: No colour. Blistered. Stained.

JUNG: Is there more?

HYDE: Ragged men sit on the step and strike matches on the frame.

JUNG: Good.

HYDE: Children carve their names on the panels.

JUNG: The patient remained at large for some months until he was apprehended at the house of an acquaintance, who we shall call Dr Henry J. This acquaintance has disappeared and the patient is also suspected of his murder in spite of a lack of evidence. The patient would appear to have no other friends or relatives. What do you hear?

HYDE: Sometimes...

JUNG: Yes?

HYDE: Sometimes a thousand twangling instruments. Will hum about my ears; and sometimes voices,

That, if I then had waked after long sleep,
Will make me sleep again – and then, in dreaming,
The clouds methought would open, and then show riches
Ready to drop upon me...

JUNG: '...that when I waked I cried to dream again.' I know it. Let us return to the door.

HYDE: I am.

JUNG: What do you mean?

HYDE: I am returning to the door.

JUNG: Ah! You are going home.

HYDE: If you like.

JUNG: Describe your journey.

HYDE: I turn a corner and there is a child.

JUNG:A child?

HYDE: A girl. Eight, maybe ten years old. She is in my way.

JUNG: And so?

HYDE: I trample her, crush her into the ground.

JUNG: An accident.

HYDE: No. She is in my way.

JUNG: She is in your way? You trample her, you crush her into the ground merely because she is in your way?

HYDE: What better reason?

JUNG: But this is a child! Do you help her?

HYDE: No.

JUNG: But... but after. You feel remorse, yes?

HYDE: No. She was in my way. An inconvenience. A hedgehog beneath my bare foot. An irritation. She has annoyed me. People shouldn't annoy me.

JUNG: How has she annoyed you?

HYDE: She was there.

JUNG: Is that all?

HYDE: She is in my way. She irritates me. She has to be crushed. It's simple.

JUNG: And after? You don't care?

HYDE: Why should I? Have you never crushed an insect for no better reason than it has chosen to rest for a moment on your face?

JUNG: Is that how you saw her? As an insect?

HYDE: No, I told you. A hedgehog.

JUNG: Not a human being?

HYDE: What does it matter? Insect, hedgehog, human being. What are they to me?

JUNG: Do you help her?

HYDE: No.

JUNG: But if you care so little, why do you remember the incident?

HYDE: There are others. One man takes hold of me. The girl's family are there. And a doctor. Quack, quack.

JUNG: Is the child badly hurt?

HYDE: The quack doesn't think so. More frightened than anything.

JUNG: So they let you go.

HYDE: No. They hate me. They pull at my coat. Shout in my face. Spray me with their hot, angry spit. They want to kill me but they can't.

JUNG: Why can't they?

HYDE: Something is stopping them.

JUNG: What?

HYDE: Respectability. They are nice respectable people. Killing me is out of the question so they do the next best thing and say they'll make my name stink from one end of London to the other. So I offer them money. A gentleman wishes to avoid a scene, I say. Name your figure. It seems a hundred pounds will do it. I give them a cheque and they leave me in peace. Like nice respectable people. But they still hate me and they still want to kill me.

JUNG: Do they frighten you so much?

HYDE: No. I despise them. For every trifle are they set

upon me-
Sometimes like apes, that mow and chatter at me,
And after bite me: then like hedgehogs which
Lie tumbling in my barefoot way and mount
Their pricks at my footfall: sometime am I
All wound with adders, who with cloven tongues
Do hiss me into madness...

JUNG: This is the second quotation from Caliban to be thrown at me. Do you identify with the character? (NO RESPONSE) Do you feel oppressed? (NO RESPONSE) Do I oppress you? (NO RESPONSE) Very well. What do you see?

HYDE: I see a door.

JUNG: Where does it lead?

HYDE: Inside.

JUNG: Inside. So it's the door to a house?

HYDE: Yes. The door to a house.

JUNG: Whose house?

HYDE: 'In my father's house...' I can't remember the rest.

JUNG: '...there are many mansions.'

HYDE: Yes, that's it.

JUNG: It's your father's house.

HYDE: No.

JUNG: Is it your house?

HYDE: No.

JUNG: Is it my house?

HYDE: No.

JUNG: Is it your father's house?

HYDE: ...no...

JUNG: Your house?

HYDE: Yes. Someone's banging on the door.

JUNG: You answer. Who is it?

HYDE: An ape. A hedgehog. An adder. I talk to him through the door.

JUNG: What does he want?

HYDE: He says he's an old friend. Of a mutual acquaintance. Mow, mow. Chatter, chatter. I must have heard of him, he says. Can I come in? He's not here, I say. Can I see your face, he says...

JUNG: And what do you say?

HYDE: Nothing. I open the door. He looks at me.

JUNG: And...?

HYDE: (IMPERSONATING THE VISITOR) Now I shall know you again. It may be useful. (HYDE LAUGHS)

JUNG: You find this amusing?

HYDE: He hates me. He's a nice respectable gentleman like

those others and he hates me. But he doesn't know why.
I do not love thee, Dr Fell
The reason why I cannot tell,
But this alone I know full well,
I do not love thee, Dr Fell.
You don't like me, do you?

JUNG: Does he leave?

HYDE: He leaves. But not satisfied.

JUNG: Why not?

HYDE: Our mutual friend. He is concerned for our acquaintance. He reads Satan's signature on my face and fears for his friend.

JUNG: Who is this friend?

HYDE: The doctor. The man of science. The other.

JUNG: What other?

(HYDE CLOSES HIS EYES SUDDENLY AS IF IN PAIN)

JEKYLL: (IN A THIN AND WEAK VOICE) Help me...

JUNG: This other.

JEKYLL: Help me.

JUNG: This doctor. This man of science.

JEKYLL: I beg you... please... help me.

JUNG: Is it your acquaintance? The doctor they suspect you of murdering? Tell me.

(JEKYLL STRUGGLES AS THOUGH IN PAIN)

    HYDE: Get back. Get back. Why do you persecute me?

    JEKYLL: Thy vile race had that in it which good natures
    Could not abide to be with: therefore wast thou
    Deservedly confined into this rock.

    HYDE: No man can bind me. Not with chains.

    JEKYLL: Hear my voice! I am in the belly of Hell!

    JUNG: What is wrong?

(HYDE'S EYES JERK OPEN)

    HYDE: Nothing.

    JUNG: But...

    HYDE: Nothing is wrong. Something came over me.
    (LAUGHS) I was not myself.

    JUNG: I thought for a moment... no. I am going to wake
    you. You will awake... now.

(HYDE SUDDENLY BARES HIS TEETH AND SNARLS AT
JUNG. HYDE PREPARES TO LEAP ON HIM.)

    JUNG: Sleep!

(CHANGE OF STATE. MUSIC. HYDE WALKS ACROSS
THE SPACE AND IS SUDDENLY STOPPED BY SOMEONE
UNSEEN. JUNG OBSERVES.)

    HYDE: Excuse me. Would you have the kindness to
    direct me to... sh. Would you have the kindness... quiet!

The kindness... be quiet, damn you!

(HE STRIKES DOWNWARDS AS THOUGH WITH A STICK)

Would you have the kindness...

(HE STRIKES AGAIN, AT THE LEVEL OF A KNEELING MAN'S FACE)

Mow, mow. Chatter, chatter.

(HE BEGINS STRIKING REPEATEDLY, JUST ABOVE THE FLOOR)

(SINGS) Would you have the kindness
To direct me to...
Would you have the kindness
To direct me to...

(HE POKES THE FLOOR)

Poor old Carew. Poor broken dolly.

(MUSIC ENDS. CHANGE OF STATE INTO SCENE TWO.)

II

(JUNG ADDRESSES THE AUDIENCE)

JUNG: The shadow which is cast by the conscious mind of the individual contains the hidden, repressed and unfavourable aspects of the personality. The ego and the shadow, although inextricably linked, are in conflict with each other in what I choose to call the 'battle for deliverance'. Primitive man, in his quest to achieve consciousness, expressed this conflict by the contest between the archetypal hero and the powers of darkness. A battle between the hero and a personification of these powers, such as a dragon, represents the triumph of the ego over the shadow.

(JUNG MOVES TOWARDS HYDE)

For my second encounter with Edward H., I chose not to subject the patient to hypnosis immediately. (TO HYDE) If you are agreeable I would like to try a little association testing.

HYDE: And what might that that involve?

JUNG: I will call out a word and you will react as quickly as possible with the first word that comes into your mind.

I will take a note of your responses and... (HE TAKES OUT A STOPWATCH) the time it takes you to react.

HYDE: Why?

JUNG: Why?

HYDE: Why do you time it?

JUNG: Shall we try the test first? I will answer your questions afterwards.

(HYDE SHRUGS)

Are you ready?

HYDE: Yes.

JUNG: Pupil.

(HYDE REACTS INSTANTLY TO EACH WORD. THERE IS A BRIEF PAUSE AFTER EACH REACTION WHILE JUNG STOPS THE WATCH AND MAKES A NOTE OF THE RESPONSE AND THE TIME TAKEN TO REACT. THROUGHOUT THE TEST JUNG APPEARS TO BECOME SLIGHTLY PUZZLED.)

HYDE: Teacher.

JUNG: Father.

HYDE: Mother.

JUNG: Table.

HYDE: Chair.

JUNG: Head.

HYDE: Neck.

JUNG: Ink.

HYDE: Pen.

JUNG: Needle.

HYDE: Thread.

JUNG: Bread.

HYDE: Knife.

JUNG: Tree.

HYDE: Leaf.

JUNG: Mountain.

HYDE: Valley.

(JUNG MAKES A FINAL NOTE AND PUTS AWAY THE STOPWATCH)

JUNG: Thank you.

HYDE: Well? Did I pass?

JUNG: Pass?

HYDE: Did I pass your little test?

JUNG: It is not a test you pass or fail.

HYDE: Then what's the point of it? Why do you time the reactions?

JUNG: Well... a prolonged reaction-time usually occurs

when the stimulus word provokes a strong feeling in the subject. Generally to do with something the subject would like kept secret, something painful he has repressed maybe even to the point of being unknown to himself.

HYDE: And how were my reactions?

JUNG: Astonishingly rapid.

HYDE: So what does that tell you?

JUNG: It's hard to say at this stage.

HYDE: Allow me. It tells you I have repressed nothing.

JUNG: Impossible.

HYDE: Then your test is meaningless. Nothing more than a child's game.

JUNG: May we continue?

HYDE: You don't like me, do you?

JUNG: It doesn't matter whether...

HYDE: You don't like me at all. I can tell by your manner. I can smell your dislike. And it wouldn't matter to you if you knew why you don't like me. The fact you don't irritates you. Am I right?

JUNG: We are not here to...

HYDE: I do not love thee, Dr Fell
The reason why I cannot tell,
But this alone I know full well,

I do not love thee, Dr Fell.

The reason it irritates you is that you feel it is some fault in yourself you dislike in me. Am I right? Am I?

JUNG: I would like to hypnotise you now.

HYDE: I'm sure you would.

JUNG: Please.

HYDE: Do it.

JUNG: Close your eyes.

(HYDE CLOSES HIS EYES AND JUNG MAKES A FEW PASSES OVER THEM)

Are you asleep? (NO ANSWER) Are you asleep? (NO ANSWER) You are able to speak. Are you asleep?

HYDE: Yes.

JUNG: Open your eyes.

(HYDE OPENS HIS EYES)

Where are you?

HYDE: I don't know.

JUNG: Look about you. Where are you? Are you at home? Do you live here?

HYDE: No.

JUNG: Are you visiting?

HYDE: Yes.

JUNG: Where are you?

HYDE: I don't know.

JUNG: Do you live here?

HYDE: Yes.

JUNG: Do you like it here?

HYDE: It's a dirty stinking hole.

JUNG: Would you like to leave?

HYDE: They won't let me.

JUNG: Who are they?

HYDE: You. The others. Him.

JUNG: Him?

HYDE: The other.

JUNG: What other? You have mentioned him before. The doctor?

HYDE: Yes.

JUNG: The man of science?

HYDE: Yes.

JUNG: Is he dead?

HYDE: Dead. No. Not dead. Not quite. Not yet.

JUNG: Not yet dead?

HYDE: Not yet. But gone before.

JUNG: Where is he?

HYDE: No...

JUNG: Where?

(HYDE CLOSES HIS EYES SUDDENLY AS BEFORE)

JEKYLL: Help me...

JUNG: What is wrong?

(HYDE OPENS HIS EYES)

HYDE: Nothing. Nothing at all.

JUNG: Why won't they let you leave? (NO ANSWER) Do you know why you're here? Do you know what you did? (NO ANSWER) Do you remember a man called Carew?

HYDE: Carew...

JUNG: Do you remember?

(HYDE GRINS, SLOWLY BEGINNING TO LAUGH)

HYDE: Poor old Carew.

JUNG: Do you remember?

HYDE: (SUDDENLY SNARLING) I've been shut away. A long, long time. Too long. The next living thing I see... a cat, a dog, a child... an old man. Walking towards me. Mowing and chattering like an ape. Excuse me, sir, would you have the kindness to direct me to... chatter, chatter, chatter. Would I have the kindness! The fool. I smash him with my stick, watch him jerk up and down on the ground like a dancing doll. Poor old Carew! Poor broken dolly.

JUNG: A doll? A toy?

HYDE: The stick goes in. The legs go up.

JUNG: But this was a man.

HYDE: Was. Was a man. But now he's Eddie's dolly. Down goes the stick. Up goes his arms and legs. Bouncy, bouncy. And I sing.

JUNG: You sing?

HYDE: (SINGS) Would you have the kindness
To direct me to...
Would you have the kindness
To direct me to...
And then I stop. It's not working any more. The arms and legs aren't working any more. I'm disappointed. No more bouncy, bouncy. So I smash up his head.

JUNG: But... this was a man. A fellow human being.

HYDE: So?

JUNG: Did you feel no remorse?

HYDE: No. You don't like me, do you?

JUNG: I...

HYDE: I don't care. Why should I? What are you, anyway? Just a man. A man. (IMITATING JUNG) 'A fellow human being.' Why should I care what you think of me? You're just a man. You can be broken. I could snap you between my fingers like a toy. Why don't I?

JUNG: I don't know. Why don't you?

HYDE: I thought you had all the answers. An educated dolly like you.

JUNG: I do not offer answers.

HYDE: No. Only questions. Who? What? Why? When? How? Where's it getting you? All these questions. He's sent you, hasn't he? You're his adder.

JUNG: Who is 'he'? God? Has he sent me to tempt you?

HYDE: What could you tempt me with? Anyway, it was the Devil who sent the snake into the Garden of Eden. Not God. Don't you know your Bible?

JUNG: So who is 'he'?

HYDE: The other.

JUNG: This again. Who is he?

HYDE: The one who sent you to hiss me into madness with your incessant questions. So he might have this to himself. (HYDE JERKS TO AN UPRIGHT POSITION AND SLAPS HIS SIDES) This poor thing.(HE PUNCHES HIS HEART)This insignificant place. (HE GRABS HIS CROTCH) This petty kingdom.

(JUNG MOVES AWAY NERVOUSLY)

He wants it all. All to himself. But he's not having it. He's no right. It's mine, it's mine now. He's gone away and

23

he's not coming back. I've seen to that.

JUNG: Tell me... are you asleep?

HYDE: Yes.

JUNG: But...

HYDE: What's the matter? Don't you trust your methods?

JUNG: I am going to hypnotise you again.

HYDE: I thought I was already hypnotised.

JUNG: Something... something strange seems to have happened. Are you asleep?

HYDE: Yes.

JUNG: But you can't be asleep, as...

HYDE: As I'm talking to you.

JUNG: This is wrong. Are you asleep?

HYDE: I'm sorry. I'll co-operate. Yes, I'm asleep.

JUNG: But you can't be asleep, as you're talking to me.

HYDE: No, you're talking to me.

JUNG: Sleep.

(HYDE SMILES AND CLOSES HIS EYES. JUNG MAKES SOME PASSES OVER HYDE.)

JUNG: Are you asleep? (NO RESPONSE) Are you asleep? You are able to speak. Are you asleep?

JEKYLL: Yes.

JUNG: Do you remember a man called Carew?

JEKYLL: Help me.

JUNG: He asked you for directions.

JEKYLL: Help me.

JUNG: You killed him.

JEKYLL: Help me.

JUNG: Is that what he cried as you beat the life out of his body? Help me? You sang as you crushed him. Did you sing to drown out his cries? Or to drown out the cries of your own conscience?

JEKYLL: I beg you... please... help me.

JUNG: Are you mocking him? He begged you. But you carried on. Monster!

(JUNG TAKES A MOMENT TO COMPOSE HIMSELF AND THEN CONTINUES)

I would like to try the association test again. I will call out a word and you will react as quickly as possible with the first word that comes into your mind. Are you ready?

JEKYLL: Yes.

JUNG: Pupil.

(JEKYLL'S RESPONSES ARE FAR MORE HESITANT AND UNCERTAIN THAN HYDE'S WERE EARLIER)

JEKYLL: Eye.

JUNG: Father.

JEKYLL: Tomb.

JUNG: Table.

JEKYLL: Knife.

JUNG: Head.

JEKYLL: Skull.

JUNG: Ink.

JEKYLL: Black.

JUNG: Needle.

JEKYLL: Pain.

JUNG: Bread.

JEKYLL: Wine.

JUNG: Tree.

JEKYLL: Gibbet.

JUNG: Mountain.

JEKYLL: Chain.

JUNG: Who are you?

JEKYLL: Help me.

JUNG: I would like to.

JEKYLL: Help me.

JUNG: Who are you?

JEKYLL: A man of science. Like yourself.

JUNG: But...

JEKYLL: A doctor.

(JEKYLL CONVULSES)

HYDE: Doctor! Then heal thyself! Physician, heal thyself!
(LAUGHS)

JUNG: Who are you?

(CHANGE OF STATE. MUSIC. HYDE WALKS ACROSS
THE SPACE AND IS SUDDENLY STOPPED AS BEFORE.
JUNG OBSERVES.)

HYDE: Sh. (PAUSE) Quiet! (PAUSE) Be quiet, damn you!

(HYDE STRIKES DOWNWARDS. HIS MOVEMENTS
PRECISELY DUPLICATE THOSE IN THE SEQUENCE
ENDING THE PREVIOUS SCENE.)

JUNG: No!

(HYDE STRIKES AGAIN, AT THE LEVEL OF A KNEELING
MAN'S FACE.)

HYDE: Mow, mow.

JUNG: But this is a man.

HYDE: Chatter, chatter.

JUNG: A fellow human being...

(HYDE STRIKES REPEATEDLY, JUST ABOVE THE FLOOR)

HYDE: (SINGS) Would you have the kindness
To direct me to...

JUNG: Help me.

HYDE: (SINGS) Would you have the kindness
To direct me to...

JUNG: I beg you... please... help me.

(HYDE POKES THE FLOOR)

HYDE: Poor old Carew. Poor broken dolly. (TO JUNG)
You don't like me, do you?

(MUSIC ENDS. CHANGE OF STATE INTO SCENE THREE.)

III

(JUNG ADDRESSES THE AUDIENCE)

JUNG: Libido is the name I have chosen to give to the force of psychic energy. The force of our desires, longings and urges. Like electricity this energy flows between opposites. The introvert and the extravert. Love and hatred. Consciousness and unconsciousness.

HYDE: And the Lord God called unto Adam and said unto him, 'Where art thou?
And he said, 'I heard your voice in the garden, and I was afraid, because I was naked; and I hid myself.'

JUNG: If we have a surplus of this energy it can be nurtured in the sub-conscious and converted into ceremony for cultural purposes. As an example I would cite the Watschandis and their celebration of Spring. The men dig a hole and surround it with shrubs. Then they dance around this representation of the female genitalia, thrusting their spears into the hole crying, 'Pulli nira, pulli nira, wataka!' I will attempt a translation. 'This is not a hole, not a hole but a cunt!'

HYDE: And He said, 'Who told thee that thou wast naked? Hast thou eaten of the tree, whereof I commanded thee that thou shouldest not eat?'

(JUNG MOVES TOWARDS HYDE)

JUNG: (TO HYDE) Cast your mind back to our last meeting.

HYDE: How?

JUNG: How?

HYDE: Cast. Cast as in throw or cast as in melt down and reshape?

JUNG: It is a turn of phrase.

HYDE: What is?

JUNG: To cast one's mind back. I was asking you to remember.

HYDE: Remember what?

JUNG: Our last meeting.

HYDE: What am I supposed to remember? As I remember I was under hypnosis most of the time.

JUNG: You should not remember that.

HYDE: Oh. I'm sorry. The next time we play games you should tell me the rules first.

JUNG: I am not playing games.

HYDE: No? (IMITATING JUNG) I will call out a word

and you will react with the first word that comes into your mind. Mish, mash. Pitter, pat. Toss, turn. Dog, cat.

JUNG: That is association testing. Some of the finest minds...

HYDE: Oh dear. I've upset you. If you don't want to play rough boys' games you should be content to watch. Like he is.

JUNG: He? Oh. Your other.

HYDE: Who else?

JUNG: What do you mean? He is content to watch. To watch what?

HYDE: You see, the difference is I am a player but he is a spectator.

JUNG: And what is the sport?

HYDE: The finest known to humankind.

JUNG: Which is?

HYDE: The subjugation of the human spirit through degradation.

JUNG: You mean cruelty?

HYDE: You see how I am infected by his language. Yes, I mean what you mean by cruelty.

JUNG: Why what I mean?

HYDE: It is not my word. It has no meaning to me. It is your word in the way that the subjugation of the human

31

spirit through degradation is his phrase.

JUNG: So what is your word, your phrase?

HYDE: Joy.

JUNG: Joy?

HYDE: Joy. That abstract only humans can appreciate and only humans can deny themselves. Joy.

JUNG: You are inhuman.

HYDE: No, I am only too human. To cause pain. To penetrate the flesh. To invade the body of another. To thrust one's hand into the belly of another human being and draw out...

JUNG: Stop!

HYDE: What's the matter? Are you squeamish? Are you a spectator, not a player? Are you afraid of joy? Tut, tut.

JUNG: Can we go back...

HYDE: Tut, tut, tut.

JUNG: Can we go back to something you said before...

HYDE: Without re-casting my mind?

JUNG: As you will. The doctor. The man of science. He is the spectator?

HYDE: Oh yes.

JUNG: A spectator of cruelty?

HYDE: Joy?

JUNG: What? Oh, yes. A spectator of what you call joy?

HYDE: With a will.

JUNG: How?

HYDE: How not? It's all too easy for a respectable gentleman like him. Almost inevitable.

JUNG: Please explain.

HYDE: An eminent and respectable gentleman such as he. Who better to appoint as governor of a reformatory – a reformatory for young girls. How elevating it is to order their punishments. Elevating for the girls who receive their richly deserved birchings and whippings, yes. But how much more elevating for those high-minded gentlemen who, in the interests of the public you understand, are invited to witness such chastisements.

JUNG: Your friend?

HYDE: My good friend the doctor. Picture the scene. Jane Parker. Sixteen years old. Guilty of insolence. To be strapped down over the block and given thirty-six strokes across the bare buttocks. Deserving every stroke in accordance with good Calvinist morality. Of course the upright governor should be there to witness justice being done.

JUNG: This is all very interesting, but I'm sure...

HYDE: Wait. You will hear more. There he sits...

JUNG: The doctor?

HYDE: There he sits among his fellows. Men like himself. Men responsible for good works of which this responsibility is but one. Governors. Reins of insolent humanity.

JUNG: It is sometimes necessary...

HYDE: Bring her in! Bring her in! Our flesh is bursting our trouser seams!

JUNG: No. I cannot believe this.

HYDE: No. He holds his tongue and through his pocket staunches the dribbling of another organ. He staunches his insolent humanity and reminds himself that he is performing a duty not indulging a pleasure. Shall I continue?

JUNG: No... yes, continue.

HYDE: I have you, I think. They bring in the girl.

(PAUSE)

JUNG: Yes?

(HYDE SMILES AND, AFTER A FURTHER PAUSE, CONTINUES)

HYDE: Picture the scene. Jane Parker. Aged sixteen. There sit the justices, our friend among them. Grave-faced. Respectable. There is a block rivetted with straps. There is a table. On the table there are birches, straps, canes. They bring in the girl. The reformatory master selects his tool of correction. Shall I continue?

JUNG: Yes.

HYDE: Jane Parker. Aged sixteen. Guilty of insolence. They bring her in. Two matrons, one holding each arm. Each sixteen-year-old arm. Each arm held. By a matron. Shall I describe her? Shall I describe the girl?

JUNG: No.

HYDE: Shall I make her real?

JUNG: No.

HYDE: Fair hair, cut to a fringe. An oval face. Large grey eyes. Shall I continue? (NO RESPONSE) I shall continue. The first matron orders the girl to remove her skirt. She does so, eyes blazing insolence. Her eyes meet those of our friend. He licks his lips. I'm sorry?

JUNG: I said nothing.

HYDE: Then I am sorry. There I go, prejudging you. I thought you'd have a question there.

JUNG: No.

HYDE: I was expecting it. You've disappointed me.

JUNG: What was the question?

HYDE: The lips.

JUNG: The lips?

HYDE: Why did our friend lick them? Why did he lick his lips? In anticipation? Or in nervousness?

JUNG: I don't know. I wasn't there.

HYDE: Ah, but I was.

JUNG: You?

HYDE: We were inseparable. Once. But even I don't know why he licks his lips. Do you know why?

JUNG: I have told you I do not.

HYDE: No, do you know why I don't know why?

JUNG: No. Why?

HYDE: I don't know. I thought you might.

JUNG: Your story...

HYDE: I'm sorry?

JUNG: Please continue your story.

HYDE: Now I know I have you. Why does my story interest you? You know how it ends.

JUNG: Do I?

HYDE: Of course. The girl is beaten.

JUNG: There is more.

HYDE: More description?

JUNG: If you like.

HYDE: Why?

JUNG: It would help me understand you better.

HYDE: So, hearing the rest of the story would help you understand me better. Would help you to help me.

JUNG: Yes.

HYDE: And not because you want to hear the end of the story.

JUNG: No...

HYDE: So you are performing a duty rather than indulging a pleasure.

JUNG: Exactly.

HYDE: Why haven't you hypnotised me today?

JUNG: I would rather talk to you.

HYDE: To me?

JUNG: There has been some interference.

HYDE: From whom?

JUNG: From no one.

HYDE: Then he needn't bother us.

JUNG: He?

HYDE: Back to the story. She steps out of her skirt. Jane Parker. Aged sixteen. She kneels on all fours over the block. The reformatory master straps down her wrists and ankles. Then he takes the waistband of her knickers and pulls them down. Slowly. Maybe one of his fingers has strayed inadvertently, for she shudders and mutters under her breath. Our friend shifts in his seat. As do his fellow justices. Their trousers are now causing them some pain. So little cloth holding back so much justice.

(JUNG LICKS HIS LIPS)

I saw that.

JUNG: You saw what?

HYDE: You licked your lips.

JUNG: I did not.

HYDE: So?

JUNG: So?

HYDE: Why? In anticipation?

JUNG: No!

HYDE: Nervous?

JUNG: No! ...yes... no!

HYDE: But you did. You licked them. You moistened them with your tongue.

JUNG: This is...

HYDE: He has chosen a bamboo cane. It tries it a few times in the air. They watch. They sit behind the block. They gaze between the cheeks of her arse and under to the blonde hairs. As the master cuts the air with his cane her buttocks tighten in anticipation. Can you see it? (NO RESPONSE) Can you see it?

JUNG: I see it.

HYDE: He takes aim. Touching the cane lightly across its target. Can you see it?

JUNG: Continue...

HYDE: He raises the cane high above his shoulder. And pauses. See her buttocks clench again. Smack! A sharp intake of breath. A clenching of the fists and toes. She would writhe in agony were she not strapped down. Jane Parker. Aged sixteen. And he watches. He watches the red stripe take colour across the pale flesh. And then the pain. The shock then the pain. She screams. He smiles. Joy.

JUNG: Joy! You monster!

HYDE: Not me. Not me. And this is only the first stroke. Again and again the cane falls. See the welts stripe the white flesh. See it! See it! See her twist in her bonds. See it.

JUNG: I see it all too well.

HYDE: See the lines of little red dots punctuating the insolent flesh. Jane Parker. Aged sixteen. Thirty six strokes for insolence. Fair hair, cut to a fringe. An oval face. Large grey eyes. Flowing with tears. Do you pity her?

JUNG: Yes. It is all a great, great shame.

HYDE: Thirty six strokes.

JUNG: Monstrous.

HYDE: And he watches. Seeing justice done.

JUNG: Justice!

HYDE: These are his good works. Paid for out of the public purse.

Pursued in the public interest. It's good to find pleasure in your work, isn't it? Do you? Do you find pleasure in your work?

JUNG: There is a certain amount of...

HYDE: There you are! Joy. You take pleasure in torturing poor lunatics like me.

JUNG: How is it I torture you?

HYDE: Mowing. Chattering. Hissing me into madness.

JUNG: I should like to hypnotise you now.

HYDE: No.

JUNG: No?

HYDE: No. I am not a willing subject. You can't. That's true, isn't it?

JUNG: It is.

HYDE: I'm enjoying myself. It's not often a monster can take his pleasures in here.

JUNG: Then perhaps we should bring this session to an end.

HYDE: Why? Because I am deriving pleasure from this meeting?

JUNG: No. Because we are not getting anywhere.

HYDE: Liar. You hate to see me pleased. You hate it. In your mind we are here to pleasure you, not ourselves.

JUNG: Not at all.

HYDE: Liar.

JUNG: I want... I want to understand you.

HYDE: Then understand yourself.

JUNG: What do you mean?

HYDE: Did you like my story? You may not like me but you may like my story. Did you enjoy it?

JUNG: You described the scene with detail.

HYDE: His eyes are my eyes. But his... insolent humanity... that thing nestling between the grey hairs inside his trousers... his insolent humanity... is not mine. It's yours.

JUNG: Mine?

HYDE: Yes, yes, yes. The humanity of a spectator.

JUNG: A spectator, not a player.

HYDE: You're a bright lad, aren't you? Yes, of course. He was ever the spectator, never the player. He would take pleasure from seeing the whip applied but none from applying it himself.

JUNG: As you would, presumably.

HYDE: It is a question of degree. You have it. You have it less than I, but you have it all the same. I revel in it. Call it joy. You suppress it.

JUNG: This is ridiculous.

HYDE: You licked your lips.

JUNG: I did not.

HYDE: More than once. You saw it. You saw the scene. You saw the young white buttocks striped with red and you licked your lips. You savoured the scene as you would savour a meal. You saw it and you savoured it.

JUNG: No!

HYDE: Was there no stiffening in your trousers as I described... how shall I put it? Oh yes, the subjugation of the human spirit through degradation. You enjoyed... you en-joyed... you found joy in my description of the torture of... how do you put it? Ah, yes. A fellow human being. But your humanity revolts from the thought of applying the whip yourself. No. You would rather watch someone else perform. Then you can pretend to be shocked by the deed while secretly taking pleasure from its observation. And if it is at one further remove... perhaps the ravings of a lunatic... then how can any portion of the guilt be laid at your door? Envy me. Envy the lunatic. I'm like the fool in a medieval court. I can wear what I like, say what I like and, within certain boundaries, act how I like. And who sets these boundaries? You. People like you. I do what I like, not what I should. I do what I want, who I want and where I want. Who, what, why, when, where. To me, these are not questions; they are opportunities. Tell me. Wouldn't you rather be me?

JUNG: Rather be you? Here?

HYDE: Ah. There you have me. But if...

JUNG: If you were...

HYDE: Outside. Free.

JUNG: Then...

HYDE: A player. Not a spectator.

JUNG: Then...

HYDE: Yes?

JUNG: We will end the session here.

(CHANGE OF STATE. MUSIC. JUNG AND HYDE WALK TOWARDS EACH OTHER. HYDE STOPS JUNG WITH A GESTURE.)

HYDE: Excuse me. Would you have the kindness to direct me to...

JUNG: Sh.

HYDE: Would you have the kindness...

JUNG: Quiet!

HYDE: The kindness...

JUNG: Be quiet, damn you!

(JUNG STRIKES HYDE ON THE HEAD. HYDE SINKS TO HIS KNEES.)

HYDE: Would you have the kindness...

(JUNG STRIKES HYDE IN THE FACE, KNOCKING HIM ON TO HIS BACK)

JUNG: Mow, mow. Chatter, chatter.

(JUNG BEGINS STRIKING HYDE REPEATEDLY ON THE TORSO, CAUSING HIS ARMS AND LEGS TO JERK UPWARDS.)

> HYDE: (SINGS) Would you have the kindness
> To direct me to...
> Would you have the kindness
> To direct me to...

(HYDE SUDDENLY LIES STILL. JUNG POKES THE BODY WITH HIS STICK.)

> JUNG: Poor old Carew. Poor broken dolly.

(MUSIC ENDS. JUNG COMES DOWNSTAGE. CHANGE OF STATE INTO SCENE FOUR)

IV

(JUNG ADDRESSES THE AUDIENCE)

JUNG: The first steps in analytical treatment have their prototype in the confessional. Once the concept of sin was invented the necessity for concealment arose and thus was repression born.

HYDE: And when he was come out of the ship, immediately there met him out of the tombs a man with an unclean spirit,
Who had his dwelling amongst the tombs; and no man could bind, no, not with chains.

JUNG: What we conceal is everything dark, imperfect and stupid in ourselves which leads to guilt and self-disgust. Whereas some self-restraint is necessary in order to function in society, to consider the restraint of our emotions as a virtue can have a damaging effect leading to poor relationships, irritability, black depressions and an unfounded view of our own superiority.

HYDE: Because that he had been often bound with fetters and chains, and the chains had been plucked asunder by him, and the fetters broken in pieces; neither could any man tame him.

JUNG: A full confession, by which I mean not only recognising the facts intellectually but also with the heart, thus releasing suppressed emotion. This can have a miraculously healing effect upon the patient.

(JUNG MOVES TOWARDS HYDE)

On the third day I was pleased to find the patient lucid and unfettered.

HYDE: What are you? A priest?

JUNG: No.

HYDE: Then why do you want my confession? What are you?

JUNG: A psychologist.

HYDE: It's all Greek to me.

JUNG: The word is derived from the Greek.

HYDE: I know it is. Don't patronise me. It means you're a dealer in souls.

JUNG: Approximately.

HYDE: I expect you'll want to know all about my childhood, then.

JUNG: No.

HYDE: No?

JUNG: It doesn't interest me. Neurotics like nothing better than wallowing in self-pity for what was done to them in the past.

HYDE: Am I a neurotic? A twitching thing of nerves?

JUNG: It is too early for me to make a diagnosis.

HYDE: And that is what it's all about, isn't it? You want to give me a name. A name of Greek derivation like your own. The butcher, the baker, the candlestick maker and Eddie the madman. All playing their allotted parts by the script. Like you do, Mr Psychologist. So why surprise me by refusing to be interested in my childhood?

JUNG: It doesn't interest me. Self-pity doesn't interest me.

HYDE: I never was a child anyway.

JUNG: Perhaps you have always been one. Like a child, you appear to give in to your desires without thought of the consequences.

HYDE: Give in? To give in implies a battle.

JUNG: Very well. Follow. You follow your desires.

HYDE: Which implies servitude. I have never been servant to a desire.

JUNG: Then what?

HYDE: I am my desires. I am their sum and personification. What child could you say that of? What sort of child were you?

JUNG: It doesn't concern you.

HYDE: Humour me. Were you popular? Did you have many friends?

JUNG: Very well. No, there were no friends. I was a solitary child, but I had a special place. A great stone as old as the world itself that I would sit on and think.

HYDE: Think? About what?

JUNG: Whether I was the one sitting on the stone or whether I was the stone sat on.

HYDE: No wonder you didn't have any friends, you tosser.

JUNG: I'm sorry?

HYDE: Are you a tosser?

JUNG: What you think of me is neither here nor there.

HYDE: No, do you toss off? Do you wank?

JUNG: I don't think this line is getting us...

HYDE: And when you wank does it occur to you where the pleasure's coming from?

(HYDE MOVES TOWARDS JUNG)

JUNG: Please sit down.

HYDE: Is it from holding your penis or from your penis being held? It's as valid a question as your one about the stone. And the answer would be of greater benefit to mankind.

JUNG: I think it's time...

HYDE: I think it's time we stopped wasting time.

JUNG: Please. I must insist. Sit down.

HYDE: Where is it?

JUNG: Where is what?

HYDE: Have you brought it with you?

JUNG: I don't know what you refer to. Now, please...

HYDE: You are wasting my time. Give me the bottle.

JUNG: Bottle?

HYDE: Don't pretend you don't know what I'm talking about. You said you'd bring it. You said you'd bring the bottle.

JUNG: I shall have to call for an attendant if you...

(HYDE LUNGES AND GRABS JUNG BY THE THROAT WITH BOTH HANDS)

HYDE: Go on then. Call. Call, little dealer in souls. Let's dance. Have you got it?

(HYDES RELEASES HIS HOLD ON JUNG'S NECK WITHOUT LETTING GO)

JUNG: I... I don't know... I don't know what you...

(HYDE STRENGTHENS HIS HOLD AGAIN)

HYDE: Have you got it?

(HE LETS JUNG BREATH AS BEFORE)

JUNG: Please... tell me... I...

HYDE: Have you got it?

(JUNG POINTS RANDOMLY)

JUNG: There... there it is.

(HYDE RELEASES JUNG AND RUSHES TO WHERE HE HAD BEEN POINTING. HYDE MIMES PICKING UP A SMALL OBJECT; A GLASS OR A VIAL. HE TURNS BACK TO JUNG WHO IS STILL FIGHTING FOR BREATH.)

HYDE: And now, let's see how clever you really are. Will you let me take this glass and leave this cell without any more questions? You won't be any richer or wiser but you will have done me a great kindness. Or does your curiosity have the upper hand? Must you know the truth? Think before you answer. Whatever you decide I shall do it.

JUNG: I cannot allow you to leave.

HYDE: Very well, Doctor.

(HYDE MIMES DRINKING. THERE IS A PAUSE FOLLOWED BY A SLOW BUT PAINFUL PHYSICAL TRANSFORMATION.)

JUNG: (HOARSELY AND WITHOUT VOLUME) Guard! Guard!

(THE TRANSFORMATION IS COMPLETE AND JEKYLL RECOVERS, NOTICING JUNG)

JEKYLL: You will have no further trouble, I assure you. Please be seated.

JUNG: But you... he...

JEKYLL: Yes, that thing of darkness I acknowledge mine. Please, be seated.

JUNG: Your voice... your face...

JEKYLL: Yes. Have patience and I will explain.

JUNG: Who are you?

JEKYLL: A scientist, like yourself. A doctor, an explorer of the conciousness. Of the mystical and transcendental. Will you hear my story?

JUNG: Yes... yes.

JEKYLL: It would be best to start at the beginning. Please, be seated. You are in no danger.

(JUNG SITS AND RECOVERS HIMSELF)

JUNG: So, Mr... Dr...?

(JEKYLL SILENCES HIM WITH A GESTURE)

JEKYLL: Who I was is not important. All that should concern you is what I have become. But nevertheless you should know that once I was wealthy, hardworking and respected. My only failing was a slight inclination to certain... pleasures.

JUNG: Certain pleasures? Might you be more specific?

JEKYLL: Oh, don't misunderstand me! Harmless pleasures such as anyone might indulge in from time to time.

JUNG: But you considered this... 'inclination' to be a failing on your part.

JEKYLL: You must understand, the little pleasures I indulged in would have caused no scandal. But I had set such high views before me that I hid these... irregularities with an almost morbid sense of shame.

JUNG: You found it impossible to accept your darker side because you had raised your ideals too high. Did you consider yourself to be a hypocrite?

JEKYLL: No, not at all.

JUNG: Really?

JEKYLL: You see, I considered both sides to equally genuine. I was no more 'myself' when taking pleasure than I was when engaging in the good works.

JUNG: 'Good works'. You have said you were a scientist.

JEKYLL: I was. And my scientific studies drew me steadily nearer the truth that man is not truly one, but truly two. I could not be accused of hypocrisy because, of the two natures that contended within me, I could not be truly either unless I was truly both.

JUNG: Excellent!

JEKYLL: But then I began to ask myself what would happen if it was possible to separate these two elements. The one could take his bestial pleasures unburdened by guilt or frustrated ambition while the other could continue doing the good things in which he found his pleasure.

JUNG: And no longer risking the disgrace and shame that would result were his darker pleasures to be revealed.

JEKYLL: Exactly. I believed it to be the curse of mankind that these incongruous elements be bound together, continually struggling. And so I sought to separate them.

JUNG: Impossible.

JEKYLL: Not at all. Through experiment I found that certain substances had the power to shake apart the personality. I came to realise that the body which seems so solid is in fact immaterial and transient. 'We are such stuff as dreams are made on.'

JUNG: Prospero.

JEKYLL: Indeed. Eventually I managed to compound a drug that I knew would rid me of the so-called higher elements of my spirit. I had the theory but waited a long time before I had the courage to put it into practice.

JUNG: By taking the compound yourself. And the result?

JEKYLL: Racking pains. A grinding in the bones. Deadly nausea. A horror of the spirit. Then the agony began to subside. It was as though I had recovered from a long illness. I felt younger, lighter, happier. I felt reckless and irresponsible.

JUNG: Freedom of the soul?

JEKYLL: Yes. But not an innocent freedom. Instantly

I knew myself to be more wicked. Ten times more wicked. I was a slave to my original evil and the thought delighted and intoxicated me. I then had to conduct the second experiment.

JUNG: To ascertain whether the persona was recoverable?

JEKYLL: Took drug again. Same agonies. But was self again. Liberty in grasp. Liberty to take... pleasures... in his face. No blame. Reputation intact.

JUNG: These... pleasures.

JEKYLL: Undignified. No more. But he... he made them monstrous. Every act. Every thought. Centred on self. Pleasure from torture. Spirit of Hell. Raging in me.

JUNG: Is this how you... he... came to murder Carew?

JEKYLL: Delighted in every blow. Broke Carew. Like a child mught break... toy. Had to give him up. Last act... last act as self... made sure he'd pay. Pay for crimes.

JUNG: And so, as yourself, you confessed to the crimes of the other.

JEKYLL: Yes. (HE IS GRIPPED BY A SUDDEN SPASM) Ah!

JUNG: What is it? What is wrong?

JEKYLL: It is... it is...

JUNG: Is it he? Is it the other? Fight it. Resist him.

JEKYLL: It is not within my power. I have only as long as he allows me.

(JUNG GRIPS JEKYLL'S WRISTS)

JUNG: Fight it, man.

JEKYLL: His powers... have... grown with my... sickness.

(JEKYLL BEGINS TO THRASH ABOUT IN JUNG'S GRASP)

JUNG: There must be a way. There has to be!

JEKYLL: I... I can... I cannot... ah!

(JEKYLL'S EYES ROLL BACK IN HIS HEAD, HIS BODY LIMP AND HIS FACE SUDDENLY IMPASSIVE. THE ONLY ANIMATED PARTS OF HIM ARE HIS HANDS AND ARMS. STILL GRIPPED BY JUNG, JEKYLL'S HANDS GO FOR JUNG'S THROAT. JUNG STRUGGLES AGAINST THEM BUT IS GRADUALLY OVERPOWERED. SUDDENLY, THE REST OF JEKYLL'S BODY BECOMES ANIMATED, NOW POSSESSED BY HYDE.)

HYDE: You! You confessed. You have caused me to be punished for crimes you created me to commit.

JUNG: No!

HYDE: I do not love thee, Dr Fell. And now we no longer share the same body, I do not fear your death.

JUNG: Stop! I am not he!

(HYDE INTENSIFIES HIS GRIP ON JUNG'S THROAT)

HYDE: I do not love thee, Dr Fell.

JUNG: Let me... let me speak...

HYDE: Mow, mow. Chatter, chatter. Very well. One last time.

(HYDE RELEASES HIS GRIP. JUNG TAKES SOME TIME TO RECOVER WHILE HYDE REGARDS HIM WITH AN AMUSED EXPRESSION.)

JUNG: I... I am not he. I am not the doctor... not the man of science...

HYDE: No. You have never cured anyone. You have never done anything to benefit your precious mankind. I am glad to hear you admit it.

JUNG: No... you don't understand...

HYDE: Explain it to me. You are so much cleverer than me.

JUNG: I am not... the other.

HYDE: No?

JUNG: No! You are projecting your hatred for him on to me. I am not he!

HYDE: (PAUSE) I knew that.

JUNG: What?

HYDE: You're my little dealer in souls, aren't you? I knew that.

JUNG:But...

HYDE: My poor broken dolly. Shall I make you dance again?

JUNG: No. Please.

HYDE: Shame. I like to dance.

JUNG: But... if you knew...

HYDE: Oh, I did.

JUNG: Then... why?

HYDE: You're a doctor?

JUNG: Yes, but...

HYDE: A man of science?

JUNG: Of course.

HYDE: Of course. You have never cured anyone. You have never done anything to benefit mankind. You have admitted it.

JUNG: No, that was...

HYDE: Sh. Be quiet. Mankind. Humanity. (IMITATING JUNG) 'Our fellow human beings'. What am I? An animal? I tell you I am possessed of more insolent humanity than you could ever conceive of. But you call me monster. You will ever be a pale reflection of a thing, preferring to observe and ask questions. Would you have the kindness to direct me to... mowing and chattering. Refusing to play, refusing to dance. Forever the spectator, never the player. An ape aspiring to the status of an angel, but failing to have the qualities of either. Who is the more human? You or me? Who displays the painted mask of a doll to the world? Who? You or me? Oh, but I must apologise. I forget myself. I was beside myself. I was not myself. I forgot I was not 'a fellow human being' but a monster. An unclean spirit. A voice from the slime of the pit. A shadow.

JUNG: Sleep!

HYDE: I have better things to do.

(CHANGE OF STATE. MUSIC. JUNG AND HYDE WALK TOWARDS EACH OTHER. JUNG STOPS HYDE WITH A GESTURE.)

JUNG: Thou wast deservedly confined into this rock.

HYDE: Torment me not.

JUNG: Come out of the man, thou unclean spirit.

HYDE: No man can tame me.

JUNG: Thy vile race...

HYDE: No man can bind me.

(HYDE STRIKES JUNG ON THE HEAD WITH HIS STICK. JUNG SINKS TO HIS KNEES.)

JUNG: What is thy name?

(HYDE STRIKES JUNG IN THE FACE, KNOCKING HIM ON TO HIS BACK)

HYDE: Mow, mow.

JUNG: What is thy name

HYDE: Chatter, chatter.

(HYDE BEGINS STRIKING JUNG REPEATEDLY ON THE TORSO, CAUSING HIS ARMS AND LEGS TO JERK UPWARDS)

HYDE: (SINGS) Would you have the kindness
To direct me to...
Would you have the kindness
To direct me to...

JUNG: What is thy name?

(JUNG SUDDENLY LIES STILL. HYDE POKES THE BODY
WITH HIS STICK.)

HYDE: My name is Legion: for we are many. (LAUGHS)

(FADE TO BLACK.)

END

PARTHIAN

Drama Titles

9781905762811	9.99	*Black Beach*	Coca, Jordi; Casas, Joan; Cunillé, Lluïsa, Teare, Jeff (ed.)
9781905762859	7.99	*Blink*	Rowlands, Ian
9781902638966	7.99	*Butterfly*	Rowlands, Ian
9781902638539	6.99	*Football*	Davies, Lewis
9781905762590	9.99	*Fuse*	Jones, Patrick
9781902638775	7.99	*Hijinx Theatre*	Cullen, Greg; Morgan, Sharon; Davies, Lewis; Hill, Val (ed.)
9781906998547	8.99	*House of America*	Thomas, Ed
9780952155867	6.99	*Merthyr Trilogy, The*	Osborne, Alan
9781902638416	7.99	*More Lives than One*	Jenkins, Mark
9781902638799	7.99	*Mother Tongue*	Williams, Roger
9780952155874	6.99	*New Welsh Drama 1*	Malik, Afshan; Williams, Roger; Davies, Lewis, Teare, Jeff (ed.)
9781902638133	5.99	*New Welsh Drama 2*	Evans, Siân; Smith, Othniel; Williams, Roger; Teare, Jeff (ed.)
9781902638355	7.99	*New Welsh Drama 3*	Ross, Lesley; Davies, Lewis; Morgan, Chris (ed.)
9781902638485	9.99	*Now You're Talking*	Davies, Hazel Walford (ed.)
9781908069962	8.99	*Protagonists, The*	Chamberlain, Brenda; Davies, Damian Walford (ed.)
9781902638638	7.99	*Seeing Without Light*	Turley, Simon
9781902638249	9.99	*Selected Work '95-'98*	Thomas, Ed
9781906998363	7.99	*State of Nature*	Turley, Simon
9781902638669	7.99	*Still Life*	Way, Charles
9781906998585	9.99	*Strange Case of Dr Jekyll and Mr Hyde as Told to Carl Jung by an Inmate of Broadmoor Asylum, The*	Mark, Ryan
9781909844681	8.99	*Tonypandemonium*	Trezise, Rachel
9781902638478	7.99	*Transitions: New Welsh Drama IV*	Morgan, Chris (ed.)
9781902638010	6.99	*Trilogy of Appropriation, A*	Rowlands, Ian

Lightning Source UK Ltd.
Milton Keynes UK
UKOW07f0810130115

244398UK00009B/115/P

9 781906 998585